IMAGES
of America

ST. LOUIS OLYMPICS 1904

I0792634

This issue of the *World's Fair Bulletin*, announcing the Olympic Games, features a portrait of Theodore Roosevelt, the honorary President of the games, flanked by laurel garlands. (St. Louis Public Library, Special Collections.)

IMAGES
of America

ST. LOUIS OLYMPICS 1904

George Matthews and
Sandra Marshall

ARCADIA
PUBLISHING

Copyright © 2003 by George Matthews and Sandra Marshall
ISBN 978-0-7385-2329-1

Published by Arcadia Publishing
Charleston, South Carolina

Printed in the United States of America

Library of Congress Catalog Card Number: 2003101016

For all general information contact Arcadia Publishing at:
Telephone 843-853-2070
Fax 843-853-0044
E-mail sales@arcadiapublishing.com
For customer service and orders:
Toll-Free 1-888-313-2665

Visit us on the Internet at www.arcadiapublishing.com

This participation medal was given to each athlete competing in any of the athletic events in St. Louis. (Greensfelder, et al.)

CONTENTS

ACKNOWLEDGMENTS

The authors want to thank these individuals and organizations for providing photographs. The Missouri Historical Society allowed access to the extensive collections housed there, and provided the majority of the photographs in this book. Jim Greensfelder, spokesman, and his three co-authors, Bob Christianson, Jim Lally, and Max Storm, gave permission to reproduce photographs from their book *1904 Olympic Games Official Medals and Badges*. Barney DePenaloza and his family shared a very special photograph of his great-grandfather, Henri de Penaloza. The Library of Congress, Prints and Photographs Division, provided the portrait of Alice Roosevelt. Special thanks goes to Jean E. Meeh Gosebrink, at the St. Louis Public Library, Special Collections, who willingly located photographs, especially from the Jessie Tarbox Beals Collection, and oversaw the reproduction of these and of photographs in the Bennitt and Sullivan books. Appreciation goes to past-president of the 1904 World's Fair Society Max Storm for his e-mail alerts to activities of the 1904 World's Fair Society and St. Louis events.

To Jessica Belle Smith, our editor at Arcadia Publishing, we express our sincere appreciation for her enthusiastic support throughout the process. More than once Jessica went above and beyond to ensure completion of this project.

The source of each photograph used in this book is cited by name, with the exception of the following four books which are cited by author:

(Bennitt.) Mark Bennitt, *History of the Louisiana Purchase Exposition*, 1905.

(Greensfelder, et al.) Jim Greensfelder, Jim Lally, Bob Christianson, and Max Storm, *1904 Olympic Games Official Medals and Badges*, 2002.

(Lucas.) Charles Lucas, *Olympic Games 1904*, 1905.

(Sullivan.) James E. Sullivan, *Spalding's Official Athletic Almanac for 1905: Special Olympic Number, Containing the Official Report of the Olympic Games of 1904*, 1905.

INTRODUCTION

America in 1904 was a nation bristling with energy and confidence. Formerly an isolationist country, the United States had recently become a recognized player on the imperialistic international stage, having flexed her muscles in the Spanish-American War. Inspired by young, energetic, and athletic President Theodore Roosevelt, a sports mania rampaged across the country. Eager to celebrate its history, and display its commercial, military, and athletic potential, the United States hosted the world at the 1904 Louisiana Purchase Exposition and welcomed the world's athletes to compete in the international Olympic Games.

The Olympic movement was also young and optimistic. The St. Louis Olympics was only the third of the modern period after the 1896 Olympic revival in Greece. Originally awarded to Chicago, the games were wrested by St. Louis from her rival city against the wishes of International Olympic Committee (IOC) President Pierre de Coubertin, and appended to the Louisiana Purchase Exposition, a world's fair celebrating the conquest of a continent.

Athletes came from 11 countries and 4 continents to compete. American athletes represented not only their country, but their particular athletic clubs, and their uniforms bore their clubs' insignia. James E. Sullivan, chief of the Physical Culture Department and director of the Olympic Games, had tried in 1901 to organize an international track and field federation in an attempt to steal control of the Olympic movement from Coubertin. The aristocratic French baron and the scrappy Irish-American mutually despised each other, causing Coubertin to withdraw his personal involvement in the games.

The elegant new gymnasium and 10,000 seat concrete stadium were state-of-the-art for the time, and sporting goods mogul Albert Spalding provided the most up-to-date physical training equipment. Olympic events began on July 1 with gymnastics and continued for nearly five months. There were 15 Olympic sports in all: gymnastics, lacrosse, rowing and sculling, cycling, track and field, weight lifting, tennis, swimming, diving, fencing, archery, golf, boxing, wrestling, and soccer. Women participated only in archery. African-Americans participated for the first time in Olympic competition; George Poage won bronze medals in the 200-and 400-meter hurdles, and Joseph Stadler won silver and bronze medals in the standing high jump and standing hop, step, and jump, respectively. The sports-happy American public all across the country followed the events, particularly track and field, in the illustrated newspapers.

The St. Louis Olympics garnered only praise at the time. American journalists were unanimous, saluting the athletes, organizers, and spectators alike. All agreed awareness of the Olympic movement and the prestige of the Games had been greatly enhanced, especially in the

United States. Even Coubertin, president of the IOC, lauded the outcome, going so far as to award Sullivan a special gold medal despite their personal animosity.

But the Olympics in London (1908) and Stockholm (1912) were even bigger and more grandiose. By 1912 the Olympic movement had achieved international acceptance and prominence only dreamed of in 1904. The St. Louis Olympics receded in memory and importance. Largely overlooked, the 1904 Games suffered an even crueler fate with the publication of Coubertin's memoirs in 1931. Almost 30 years after the event, with the luxury of the Olympics established as an international success, Coubertin was still unhappy about the transfer of the games and, unable to put aside his personal resentment toward James Sullivan, he unfairly and inaccurately labeled the St. Louis Olympics a failure. Coubertin charged that the Games had been overshadowed by the World's Fair. Even more damning, he accused American Olympic officials of perpetrating a painful episode called "Anthropology Days," wherein so-called "primitive peoples" competed against one another in European-style sports for the amusement of Anglo-Saxon spectators.

Subsequent harsh judgment has been based more often on these spiteful memoirs than on primary documentation. In fact, as an adjunct to the World's Fair, the Olympic Games received enthusiastic official support and broader public exposure. In addition, Anthropology Days was not part of the Olympics, but one of three similar exhibitions, including "Barbarian Days" and "Philippine Tribal Contests" organized by the World's Fair Department of Anthropology. The 1904 St. Louis Olympics should more accurately be remembered as the Games where African-Americans competed and medaled for the first time, and as a time when international participation, a high caliber of athletic competition, and the interest and support of the American public—spurred by newspaper coverage—helped secure the future of the young Olympic movement.

One

Ceremonies and Celebrities

ST. LOUIS GETS OLYMPIC GAMES

International Committee Sanctions the Change for the World's Fair in 1904.

ST. LOUIS, Mo., Feb. 11.—"Everything settled. You have Olympic games," is the wording of a cablegram received to-day from Michel La Grave, Wold's Fair Commissioner at Paris, France, by the Louisiana Purchase Exposition officials.

The meaning of the cablegram is that the Olympic Games, which were originally intended to be held in Chicago in 1904, will be held in St. Louis during the World's Fair, the International Committee having so decided.

Headlines in the February 12, 1903 *New York Times* announce that the International Olympic Committee has officially transferred the 1904 Olympic Games from Chicago to St. Louis. (*New York Times*.)

In 1893, then Missouri Governor David R. Francis lost a bid for the Columbian quarter-centenary world's fair to Chicago. As president of the Louisiana Purchase Centennial Exhibition he was determined to capture the 1904 Olympics for St. Louis. It was he who sent a personal envoy, the mysterious Count Henri de Penaloza, to International Olympic Committee President Pierre de Coubertin in 1901 with an unofficial request that the Olympics be awarded to St. Louis. At the time of this request, the World's Fair was still supposed to take place in 1903. Francis had not yet petitioned Congress for a year's postponement until 1904, the same year the Olympics would be held. Although Francis had little personal interest in athletics, the influential businessman and politician recognized the popular enthusiasm for sports at the turn of the 20th century. He also served as president of the 1904 Olympic Games, presided at the May 14 opening ceremonies, and commissioned a silver cup for the winner of the marathon, for which he fired the starting pistol. (Sullivan.)

Francis hired Frederick J.V. Skiff, who directed the Field Columbian Museum for the 1893 Chicago World's Fair, as director of exhibits for the St. Louis Exposition. Skiff's telephone call to fellow Chicagoan and sporting equipment mogul Albert Spalding to request a transfer of the games, as well as subsequent persuasive correspondence with the Chicago Olympic Committee, assured the relocation of the Olympics to St. Louis. (Sullivan.)

A French count—but a resident of St. Louis between 1897 and 1904—Henri de Penaloza met with Coubertin in Paris in April 1901. David Francis had asked Penaloza to make an unofficial request on behalf of St. Louis for the 1904 Olympic Games. Married to Marie Fusz in 1897, he was the son-in-law of Louis Fusz, prominent St. Louis businessman and fellow member, with Francis, of the Merchants Exchange Club. (Barney DePenaloza and family.)

Alfred L. Shapleigh, in his starched wing collar and three-piece suit, was the chairman of the Physical Culture Committee and assisted Skiff in securing the Olympics for St. Louis. It was Skiff's idea to create a separate Department of Physical Culture for the Exposition, reflecting America's preoccupation with sports and athletics. (Sullivan.)

Pressing a golden telegraph key in St. Louis, David R. Francis signals to President Theodore Roosevelt at the White House that the Louisiana Purchase Exposition is officially open. (Missouri Historical Society.)

Jessie Tarbox Beals, wearing a duster and her perpetually enthusiastic expression, stands beside, and nearly under, her camera with the shutter release bulb in her upraised hand. Her assistant, whom she called "Punkin" for his ruddy cherubic face, carried the heavy case full of glass plates. (Missouri Historical Society.)

"Always smiling and so beguiling," jovial Secretary of War William Howard Taft is photographed by Jessie Tarbox Beals at the Louisiana Purchase Exposition opening day ceremonies on April 30. Taft was President Roosevelt's official representative on this day; in 1908, he succeeded Roosevelt for one term as President. (Missouri Historical Society.)

Alice Roosevelt, daughter of the President, made two separate visits to the St. Louis World's Fair. Frances Benjamin Johnston, a female professional photographer, took this portrait. Legend has the lovely and sought-after Miss Roosevelt awarding medals to the young and handsome international Olympic champions. Actually, Alice handed out medals on one day, June 4, and only to American track and field athletes competing in the Amateur Athletic Union Championships. (Library of Congress, Prints and Photographs Division.)

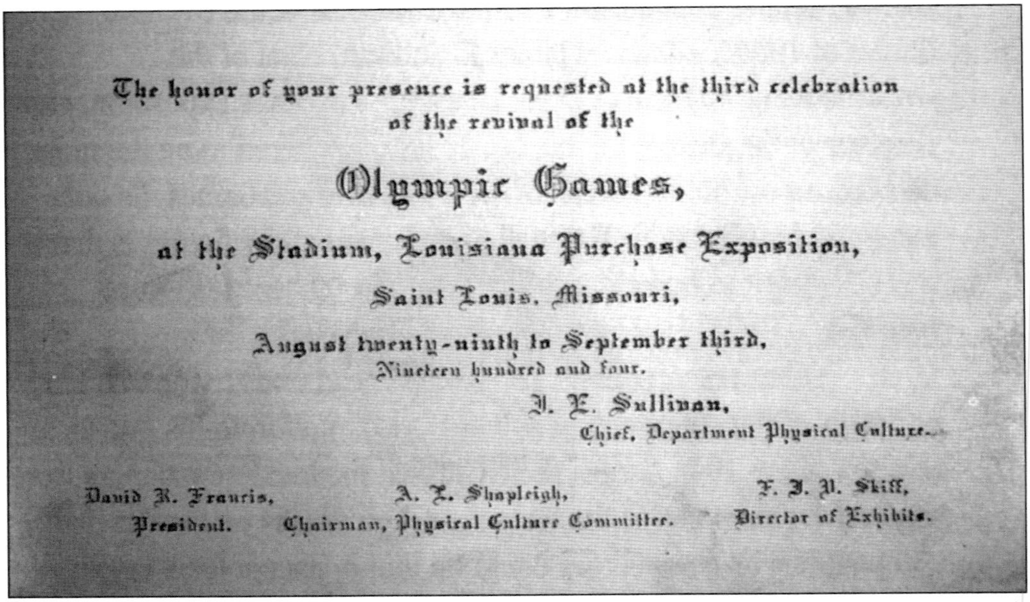

The honor of your presence is requested at the third celebration of the revival of the

Olympic Games,

at the Stadium, Louisiana Purchase Exposition,

Saint Louis, Missouri,

August twenty-ninth to September third,
Nineteen hundred and four.

J. E. Sullivan,
Chief, Department Physical Culture.

David R. Francis,
President.

A. L. Shapleigh,
Chairman, Physical Culture Committee.

F. J. V. Skiff,
Director of Exhibits.

An official invitation to the Olympic Games (track and field), held August 29 through September 3, was sent out by James E. Sullivan, chief of the Department of Physical Culture and director of the Olympic Games. (Greensfelder, et al.)

Secretary of State John Hay, resplendent in a silk hat and distinguished white beard, is literally looked up to by the crowd at the April 30 opening ceremonies of the Louisiana Purchase Exposition. A line of tall policemen and short, but stern, military cadets separates the officials from the spectators. Later, Hay served as President Roosevelt's official representative at the May 14 opening ceremonies of the Olympic Games. (Missouri Historical Society.)

Officials of the Olympic Games pictured here are: Clark Hetherington (3), well-known physical educator from Missouri; Canadian R. Tait McKenzie (8), an artist as well as a physical educator; Francis Kemeny (21), a member of the International Olympic Committee and leader of the Austrian delegation, who represented the IOC in the absence of Coubertin; C.J. Harvey (39), with megaphone in his lap was the announcer for the track and field events. James E. Sullivan (35), director of the 1904 Olympic Games, dominates the photograph even behind a post. Sullivan was the czar of American athletics until his death in 1914, heading Olympic delegations in 1906, 1908, and 1912. (Bennitt.)

Athletic facilities were state of the art. Washington University built the stadium, gymnasium, and grounds for initial use by the Exposition, and leased them for the duration of the Fair. A pole-vaulter relaxes with his pole in the lower left, behind the long jump and pole vault pits. Shot put and discus throwing areas are in the center of the field. A high-jumper, caught in midair in the foreground of the picture, performs before officials in what was likely the standing high jump competition. (Lucas.)

In 1901, as part of a capital campaign to build their new campus, Washington University leased about 600 acres and several already completed buildings to the World's Fair for $650,000, plus an extra $100,000 when the Fair was delayed to 1904. This money funded construction of the stadium and Physical Culture Building, pictured here nearing completion. These facilities became a permanent part of Washington University campus after the Olympics. Now called Francis Field and Gymnasium, they are still in use today. (Missouri Historical Society.)

A good stadium crowd awaits the beginning of Olympic Games competition. The section numbers are clearly visible on the front of the concrete wall, and extra chairs fill the aisle to the right. (Bennitt.)

The use of "Olympic Games" on this medal given for the Western Intercollegiate Championships shows the multiple use of the term for a variety of athletic competitions in St. Louis. (Greensfelder, et al.)

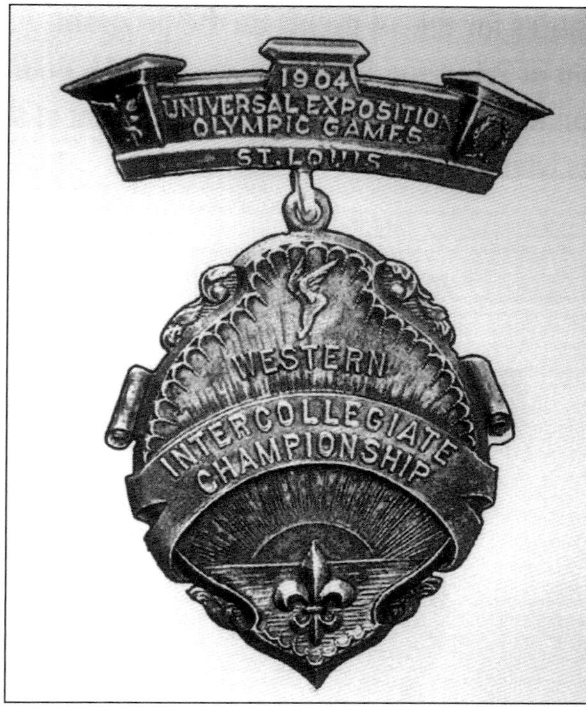

The Greek delegation poses outside of the Physical Culture building. Standing, left, is Perikles Kakousis, gold medalist in weightlifting, and right, Nilolaos Georgantas, discus bronze medalist. Seated, left, is D. Jannopoulo, Greek Consul in St. Louis, and right, H.E.M. Pasmezoglu, secretary for the Greek delegation. (Lucas.)

This design was cast in gold, silver, and bronze, and presented to the first, second, and third place winners in each event. The name of the event was inscribed on the reverse. (Greensfelder, et al.)

Germany's athletes and members of the delegation pose in street clothes on the life saving exhibit dock. A boat used in life saving drills is behind them. Identified by numbers in 1904, this information is now lost. The two dapper gentlemen, standing on either end, appear to be leaders of the German delegation. (Missouri Historical Society.)

Two

Track and Field

Running Events

At the start of the first heat of the 60-meter race, George Poage, the first African American to compete in an Olympic Games, is second from the right. Poage represented the Milwaukee Athletic Club and was a student at the University of Wisconsin. (Missouri Historical Society.)

A good crowd watches Archie Hahn of the Milwaukee Athletic Club easily win the third heat of the 60-meter sprint. Pictured here from left to right are Lawson Robertson, Greater Irish New York Athletic Club; Robert Kerr, Canada; Hahn with arms raised; and Béla de Mezo, Hungary. Mezo, unable to understand English commands, made two false starts and was about to be disqualified when American runners Hahn and Robertson intervened and insisted that Mezo be allowed to compete. Franz Kemeny, leader of the Hungarian Olympic delegation and member of the IOC, publicly commended this display of sportsmanship. (Missouri Historical Society.)

At the starting line of the 60-meter sprint, the runner with the best form, second from the left, is the winner Charles Archibald "Archie" Hahn. Competing in the track and field events were 142 athletes from 10 countries.(Missouri Historical Society.)

At the finish of the 60-meter sprint, Archie Hahn, the winner in 7 seconds flat, is on the far left. Hahn's speed earned him the nicknames "Milwaukee Meteor" and "Wisconsin Wonder." (Missouri Historical Society.)

Archie Hahn wins the final heat and the gold medal for the 100-meter sprint. Hahn became a track coach at Princeton and later at the University of Virginia. His book, *How to Sprint*, is considered a classic. (Missouri Historical Society.)

Director of Exhibits Frederick J.V. Skiff, looking natty in pinstripes, presents the Skiff Cup to Archie Hahn for winning the 100-meter sprint. (Missouri Historical Society.)

Archie Hahn stands amid clumps of weeds and grass in the rough infield of the stadium holding the Skiff Cup he won for the 100-meter sprint. Although only 5-feet, 6-inches tall, Hahn was a triple gold medalist, winning the 60, 100, and 200-meter sprints. He won the 100-meter sprint again at the 1906 Athens Olympics, becoming the only athlete to win consecutive 100-meter events until Carl Lewis's performances in 1984 and 1988. (Missouri Historical Society.)

Fashionably dressed spectators in the more expensive center sections of the stands smile and chat as they watch the competitions. These sections offered individual wooden chairs with backs; the rest of the stadium seating was only backless concrete bleachers. The four rows of plank tables in the reporters' section to the left make it easier for them to take notes. A carved, high-backed distinguished visitor's chair stands empty in the first row. On this sunny day, spectators hold umbrellas and parasols for shade, and the woman in the front row is swathed in a veil. (Missouri Historical Society.)

A determined-looking Archie Hahn, 24, lines up at the far right for the final heat of the 200-meter race. Tape stretched from one end of the course to the other marks the lanes, and the starter, pistol in hand, stands on a fence rail. Hahn's time, 21.6 seconds, set an Olympic record that held until 1932. (Missouri Historical Society.)

At the finish of the 400-meter run, Harry L. Hillman of the New York Athletic Club leads the field. There were 12 separate running events: 60, 100, 200, 400, 800 and 1500-meter runs, 110, 200, and 400-meter hurdles, a steeplechase, a 4-mile team race, and the marathon. (Missouri Historical Society.)

The 12-man field is crowded at the start of the 400-meter run. George Poage is third from the right with number 170 on his back. The starter, pistol in hand, stands on a fence rail. The American flag at left is inside the Aeronautical Concourse, behind the wooden fence and the high windscreens. (Missouri Historical Society.)

Harry Hillman seems to be catching his breath. Hillman won three gold medals, for the 200-meter hurdles, the 400-meter hurdles, and the 400-meter run. He also competed in Olympic Games in Athens (1906) and London (1908). In 1910, he began a distinguished 35-year coaching career at Dartmouth College. (Missouri Historical Society.)

Thirteen runners take off at the start of the 800-meter race. Winner James D. Lightbody of the Chicago Athletic Association is sixth from the left. The tall wooden windscreens in the background surround the Aeronautical Concourse. (Missouri Historical Society.)

At the halfway mark of the 800-meter run, James Lightbody, the eventual winner, is in forth position. Lightbody made his move, coming up on the outside in the final stretch, and won by two yards. (Missouri Historical Society.)

The aptly named James Lightbody won three gold medals for the 800-meter run, the 1500-meter run, and the 2590-meter steeplechase, and a silver for the 4-mile team race. (Missouri Historical Society.)

Lightbody receives the Gregg Souvenir Cup from A.L. Shapleigh, chairman of the Exposition's Physical Culture Committee, after winning the 1500-meter race on Saturday, September 3. The cup, donated by Director of Division, Concessions and Admission Norris B. Gregg, was one of several commissioned by prominent businessmen and boosters for various events. Lightbody, 22, also placed first in the 800-meter race and the 2590-meter steeplechase. The photographer was Jessie Tarbox Beals. (Missouri Historical Society.)

James Lightbody, with a big smile on his face, easily wins the 1500-meter run. (Missouri Historical Society.)

In this non-Olympic event, the 100-yard handicap race, the runners are staggered at their starting lines. This allowed less gifted athletes a chance to be competitive against world class runners. (Missouri Historical Society.)

Johannes Runge of Germany understood little English and spoke less. He entered the first event of the track and field competition, the 880-yard handicap race, on August 29, not realizing it was a non-Olympic event. Runge won the race, but no Olympic medal. He later finished fifth in the Olympic 800-meter race. (Lucas.)

Johannes Runge assumes something like a running pose and stares into the sun as a photographer, casting a shadow on the foreground, takes his picture. Runge finished fifth in both the 1500-meter and 800-meters runs, and competed, but did not place, in the 400-meter run. (Missouri Historical Society.)

Amos Alonzo Stagg, far right, poses with his University of Chicago track team in St. Louis. Stagg, an accomplished track and field coach, had also taken a team to the 1900 Paris Olympics, but later achieved his greatest fame as a legendary football coach. (Sullivan.)

Pictured here in the final heat of the 110-meter hurdles, from left to right, are Fred Schule, Milwaukee Athletic Club, first place; Frank Castleman, Greater New York Irish Athletic Association, fourth; Lesley Ashburner, Yale University, third; and Thaddeus Shideler, Chicago Athletic Association, second. (Missouri Historical Society.)

A mostly male crowd watches the second heat of the 110-meter hurdles. Leslie McPherson, in the dark jersey, and his teammate Corrie Gardner, representing the Melbournian (Australia) Hare and Hounds Athletic Club, both competed in the 110-meter hurdles and the broad jump, but neither medaled. Frank Castleman, winner of this heat, is visible over the shoulder of Chicagoan Thaddeus Shideler, silver medalist in the championship heat. (Missouri Historical Society.)

Fred W. Schule of the Milwaukee Athletic Club won the gold in the 110-meter hurdles. He also competed in the 200-meter hurdles, but only finished in fifth place. (Missouri Historical Society.)

In the 200-meter hurdle race held on Thursday September 1, winner Harry Hillman, 23, sails over a 2-foot, 6-inch high hurdle, ahead of African-American George Poage, as spectators watch from the second floor of the Physical Culture Building. Unlike modern hurdles that right themselves if knocked over, these are stationary. The height is changed by removing the cotter pin (the dark rod), moving the interior square frame up or down, and reinserting the pin in a new alignment of holes in the frame and base. (Missouri Historical Society.)

Spectators leaning on the railing and out of windows watch the finish of the 200-meter hurdle race. Pounding down the straight-away next to the Physical Culture Building are the winner Harry Hillman Jr. of the New York Athletic Club, just seen at far left; Frank Castleman of the Greater New York Irish Athletic Association, far right, placing second; and George Poage of the Milwaukee Athletic Club, center, coming in third. (Bennitt.)

Opposite, Top: Jessie Tarbox Beals photographed the finish of the third heat of the 100-yard handicapped trials. The winner, James D. McGann of the Chicago Central YMCA, had been given a 4-yard advantage. The west end of the Physical Culture Building is in the background. (St. Louis Public Library, Special Collections.)

Opposite, Bottom: Harry Hillman wins the 400-meter hurdles; Frank Waller of the Milwaukee Athletic Club comes in second. Behind and left, Waller's teammate and University of Wisconsin student George Poage finishes third. On the previous Monday, Poage became the first African American to compete in the Olympics as a participant in the 60-meter sprint. This afternoon, he and Joseph Stadler, second place winner in the standing high jump, became the first African Americans to medal. (Missouri Historical Society.)

Runners in the team relay race (now called cross-country) line up for the last event in the Olympic track and field competition. Only two teams competed, the Chicago Athletic Association and the New York Athletic Club. Going into this final event, Chicago held a slight lead in team points, but the team that won this race would receive the Spalding Victory Cup for the overall Olympic track and field team championship. New York won the race and the championship by one point. (Lucas.)

Three

Track and Field

Field Events

Ward McLanahan of the New York Athletic Club and a student at Yale University clears the bar at 11 feet. McLanahan finished fourth in the pole vault and also competed in the 110-meter hurdles. (Missouri Historical Society.)

After clearing the bar, Charles Edward Dvorak, 25, of the Chicago Athletic Association, pushes his pole away and falls toward the sand pit. (Bennitt.)

Charles Dvorak heads up and over the bar as officials and a Chicago Athletic Association teammate watch his technique. (Missouri Historical Society.)

Dvorak sails through the air, winning the pole vault competition for the Chicago Athletic Association on September 3. The winning height was 11 feet, 6 inches. The pole vault was one of 12 field events, which included the following: the high jump; standing high jump; broad jump; standing broad jump; tug-of-war; hop, step, and jump; standing hop, step, and jump; shot put; discus; hammer throw; and 56-pound weight throw. (Missouri Historical Society.)

Charles Dvorak, standing on the boardwalk in front of the dignitaries' grandstand box, receives the Baxter Cup for placing first in the pole vault. (Missouri Historical Society.)

Pictured here is Dvorak after winning the pole vault. This was his specialty and the only event in which he participated. (Missouri Historical Society.)

Judges watch as Greek athlete Nikolaos Georgantas hurls the discus. The tape measure dangles from the shirt-sleeved judge's hand and snakes across the ground. Georgantas's distance of 123 feet, 7.5 inches earned him the bronze medal. He also competed in the shot put and as a member of the Greek tug-of-war team. (Missouri Historical Society.)

Ralph Rose, 20, of the Chicago Athletic Association, throws the discus. He competed in all the throwing events, including the 56-pound weight throw and the hammer, losing the discus to Martin Sheridan, but winning his first gold in shot put. (Missouri Historical Society.)

Tape measure at the ready, the shirt-sleeved official prepares to measure Martin J. Sheridan's discus throw. Sheridan, 23, of the Greater New York Irish Athletic Association, won the gold with a throw of 128 feet, 10.5 inches. (Missouri Historical Society.)

Standing at the rear of an iron ring, Irish immigrant Martin J. Sheridan prepares to throw the discus. After six throws a piece, he was tied with shot-put medalist Ralph Rose. Given three more throws each, Sheridan won with a distance of 127 feet, 10.25 inches, beating Rose by 7 feet, 3.5 inches. An outstanding athlete, Sheridan participated in several Olympiads, winning a total of nine medals, including five gold, before his untimely death in 1918. (Missouri Historical Society.)

John Flanagan of the Greater New York Irish Athletic Association winds up to throw the discus. Although he placed fourth in this event, he won first in the hammer throw and second in the 56-pound throw. (Missouri Historical Society.)

For winning the discus throw, Martin J. Sheridan receives a victory cup from donor Isaac S. Taylor, a World's Fair administrator. President Francis, left, in the expansive white shirt front, observes. (Bennitt.)

Martin Sheridan competed in three Olympiads. In St. Louis he won his first gold medal in the discus event. (Missouri Historical Society.)

The Milwaukee Athletic Club, left, faces the St. Louis Turners #1 in the tug-of-war. To win, a 5-member team pulled the opposition 6 feet; if neither team pulled the distance within the 5-minute time limit, the side that pulled the furthest won. Milwaukee hauled St. Louis six feet in 1 minute, 44 seconds, and went on to defeat the New York Athletic Club for the gold medal. (Missouri Historical Society.)

A judge, kneeling in the white shirt, watches to proclaim the winner of this tug-of-war match. The anchor man has the rope looped around his waist and his feet firmly dug into the ground. St. Louis #1, on the left, beat St. Louis #2 in this match and went on to finish second overall. (Missouri Historical Society.)

The Milwaukee Athletic Club tug-of-war team is pictured here. From left to right are Henry Sieling, Conrad Magnussen, Patrick Flanagan, Sidney B. Johnson, and Oscar Olson. The team beat South Africa, St. Louis Turners #1, and the New York Athletic Club to win the gold. The pads on the shoulders and upper arms protect from rope burns. (Missouri Historical Society.)

The St. Louis Turners #1, on the right, beat the Greek team, on the left, eliminating them from the tug-of-war competition. St. Louis #1 team members are Max Braun, William Seiling, Orrin Upshaw, Charles Rose, and August Rodenberg. On the Greek team are Nikolaos Georgantas, Perikles Kakousis, Dimitrios Dimitiakopoulos, Anastasios Georgopoulos, and Vasilios Metalos. The Physical Culture Building stands in the background. (Missouri Historical Society.)

Weightlifting officials in the background sneak a peek at Fred Englehardt of the Mohawk Athletic Club of New York as he competes in the hop, step, and jump event. Englehardt won the silver medal with a distance of 45 feet, 7.25 inches. He also competed in the running broad jump, finishing fourth. (Missouri Historical Society.)

Shirt-sleeved officials watch Robert S. Stangland of the New York Athletic Club take third in the running broad jump with a distance of 22 feet, 7 inches. Stangland also won the bronze in the running hop, step, and jump (triple jump). (Missouri Historical Society.)

Myer Prinstein of the Greater New York Irish Athletic Association wins the running broad jump (now called the long jump) with a leap of 24 feet, 1 inch. (Missouri Historical Society.)

Airborne Myer Prinstein wins the gold medal for the running hop, step, and jump with a distance of 47 feet, 1 inch. The event judge, seated with cigar in hand, watches for foot faults and prepares to mark the jump. The suited official with the tape will measure and announce the distance. This was Prinstein's second gold medal; the first was for the running broad jump. Fred Winters, in his long underwear and unique shin guards, lifts weights in the background. (Missouri Historical Society.)

Pictured here is Myer Prinstein, winner of two Olympic gold medals, in the running broad jump and the running hop, step, and jump. Prinstein also competed in the 60-meter sprint and took fifth in the 400-meter race. (Missouri Historical Society.)

Standing 6 feet, 6 inches and weighing 265 pounds, Ralph Rose was a giant in his day. He was a triple medalist: gold for shot put, silver for discus, and bronze for the hammer throw. (Missouri Historical Society.)

Ralph Waldo Rose of the Chicago Athletic Association prepares to throw the shot put. Rose reigned as the shot put king for 19 years, setting the world record four times between 1907 and 1909. His best distance was 51 feet, .75 inches. (Missouri Historical Society.)

Ralph Rose heaves the 16 pound shot as Judge Martin Delaney watches. Rose managed his best distance of 48 feet, 7 inches to win the gold on his last attempt. (Missouri Historical Society.)

Ray Ewry of the New York Athletic Club prepares to execute the standing broad jump. The crouching judge watches for a possible foot-fault, and the two with the tape are ready to measure the distance. The umbrella, used as a stake, is stuck into the ground. (Missouri Historical Society.)

Samuel J. Jones, using the scissors technique, wins the running high jump with a height of 5 feet, 11 inches. Jones, 25, represented the New York Athletic Club and was the Amateur Athletic Union high jump champion in 1901, 1903, and 1904. He also competed in the tug-of-war and came in seventh in the hop, step, and jump. (Missouri Historical Society.)

Ray Ewry, winner of three gold medals, sports the New York Athletic Club foot of Mercury on the front of his jersey. (Missouri Historical Society.)

Ray Ewry executes the scissors technique to win the standing high jump with a leap of 5 feet, 3 inches. Joseph Stadler, an African American representing the Franklin Athletic Club of Cleveland, won the silver in this event. On the same day, George Poage won the bronze in the 400-meter hurdles, making Stadler and Poage the first two African Americans to win Olympic medals. (Lucas.)

Long, lean Ray Ewry won the gold in three standing jump events. He won the same three events at the 1900 Paris Olympics; the French nicknamed him "The Human Frog." (Missouri Historical Society.)

Étienne Desmarteau of the Montreal Athletic Association winds up to throw the 56-pound weight. His winning distance of 34 feet, 4 inches went a foot further than the second place distance. (Missouri Historical Society.)

Étienne Desmarteau became Canada's first Olympic track and field champion, winning the 56-pound weight throw. A policeman, Desmarteau lost his job when he insisted on going to St. Louis. After winning the gold medal, he was reinstated. (Missouri Historical Society.)

John Flanagan of the Greater New York Irish Athletic Association holds the 16-pound hammer he threw to win the gold medal. He had previously placed first in this event in the 1900 Paris Olympics. (Missouri Historical Society.)

John Flanagan throws the 56-pound weight. The 31-year-old policeman placed second; his 33-foot-4-inch-distance fell one foot short of the mark set by another policeman, Canadian Étienne Desmarteau. Flanagan's best event was the hammer throw; he also won Olympic gold in Paris in 1900 and in London in 1908. Scurrying along in the background are photographer Jessie Tarbox Beals and her equipment-toting assistant. (Missouri Historical Society.)

John Flanagan, revolving in the 7-foot throwing circle, is about to release the 56-pound weight. Flanagan won the silver medal in this event. (St. Louis Public Library, Special Collections.)

The handsome victory cup, donated by sporting goods magnate Albert G. Spalding, displays the winged foot of the Greek god Mercury. This trophy went to the New York Athletic Club, the overall winning team of the Olympic track and field events that took place between August 29 and September 3. (Greensfelder, et al.)

Four

A Peculiar Marathon

The Greek marathoners, accompanied by Cuban Felix Carbajal (#3), pose for a group photograph. In order to compete, Carbajal, the 5-foot-tall former mailman, raised funds by giving running demonstrations in Cuba, once running the entire length of the island. En route to St. Louis, he lost all of his money in a New Orleans dice game, and walked, occasionally hitchhiking, the rest of the way. (Missouri Historical Society.)

South African Tsuana tribesmen Len Tau (left) and Jan Mashiani (right)attended the World's Fair as part of the Boer War exhibit. Both had been long distance message runners in the recent hostilities. Entered in the marathon, Tau finished ninth and Mashiani twelfth. Newspapers reported that Tau was chased nearly a mile off course by a dog, losing six or seven minutes. Some accounts also claimed that both ran barefoot, although in this photograph Tau wears shoes. (Missouri Historical Society.)

Marathoners receive last minute instructions from straw-hatted officials. One runner props his foot against the rail to tie his shoelace. Many of the participating Olympians in 1904 did not wear socks. The marathon was the only event scheduled for August 30, and it began at 3 p.m. in the afternoon, in 90-degree heat. Runners from Cuba, Greece, South Africa, and the United States participated. (Missouri Historical Society.)

Marathon runners line up to begin the race. An official, center in straw-hat, makes his way through the runners to help start the race. Of the 32 starters, only 14 finished. Thomas Hicks, #20, of the Cambridge, Massachusetts YMCA, won in 3 hours, 29 minutes, after a grueling ordeal. Albert Cory, #7, of the Chicago Athletic Association, was second, and Arthur Newton, #12, New York Athletic Club, came in third. (Lucas.)

Smoke from the starting pistol fired by David Francis partially obscures spectators in the stands as the grueling marathon begins. A few of the starters concentrate on the course in front of them, but most stare at Francis. Fred Lorz of the Mohawk Athletic Club of New York, #31, second from the left, darts between Hicks, right, and #39, Sidney Hatch of the Chicago Athletic Association, on the left. (Missouri Historical Society.)

The front five marathoners after the first lap around the third-of-a-mile-long stadium track are seen here. Winner Thomas Hicks is now fourth. Frank Pierce (#9), an American Indian and a member of the Pastime Athletic Club of New York, leads. Number 12 is third-place finisher Arthur Newton. Harry Jenakas of Greece is #32, and #10, Sam Mellor of the Mohawk Athletic Club, follows Hicks. (Missouri Historical Society.)

Fred Lorz leads at the end of the third lap around the track before heading out into the countryside. Suffering from severe cramps at the 9-mile mark, Lorz got into an automobile and rode for a few miles. Feeling better, he got out and began running again. (Sullivan.)

Four marathon officials prepare to follow the runners along the course. Charles J.P. Lucas, author of *The Olympic Games 1904*, is seated on the right in the front seat. Lucas saw Fred Lorz riding in the automobile. Later, when Lorz began running again and passed leader Thomas Hicks, Lucas disqualified him and ordered him off the course. (Lucas.)

12

12
RYE

Felix Carbajal, possibly the best athlete in the marathon, runs in street shoes, long pants cut off at the knees, a long-sleeved shirt, and a beret. Despite his attire and stops along the route to chat in broken English with spectators and eat peaches playfully snatched from an official's party, Carbajal came in fourth. Had he not stopped, he probably would have won, setting a world's record. (Missouri Historical Society.)

Opposite, Top: A bicyclist and an automobile carrying marathon officials follow two unidentified runners over the dusty course. Although disqualified, Lorz continued running into the stadium and, for a moment, the crowd thought he had won. Lorz claimed it was just a joke, but the Amateur Athletic Union barred him from competition for life. He was later reinstated and won the Boston Marathon in 1905. (Missouri Historical Society.)

Opposite, Bottom: At the six-mile mark, the three lead runners, closely followed by two bicyclists, are the following: Sam Mellor, #10, of the Mohawk Athletic Club; Edward P. Carr, #11, of the Xavier Athletic Club of New York; and Arthur Newton, # 12, of the New York Athletic Club. Mellor and Carr eventually dropped out, while Newton finished third. Newton had also run the marathon in the 1900 Paris Olympics. (Missouri Historical Society.)

Half way through the marathon, Sam Mellor leads the field. A short time later, Mellor, winner of the 1902 Boston Marathon, suffered severe cramps, slowed to a walk, then dropped out. Twelve automobiles carrying officials and physicians accompanied the runners over the dirt course, raising clouds of choking dust. Mellor suffered no permanent harm; he lived to be 92 years old. (Missouri Historical Society.)

Twenty-nine-year-old Thomas Hicks leads the marathon at the 20-mile mark, passing cornfields on the right and running into the cloud of dust raised by automobiles ahead of him. (Missouri Historical Society.)

Winner Thomas Hicks receives assistance and a sponge bath along the course from race officials. Hicks suffered a grueling ordeal in the last 10 miles of the race. Requesting water, he was denied; only his lips were dampened with a sponge. Reaching a state of near exhaustion at seven miles from the stadium, he was given one-sixtieth of a grain of strychnine and egg white as stimulants. Four miles from the stadium, Hicks asked to lie down, but his handlers allowed him only to slow, briefly, to a walk. Resuming a slow trot and suffering from fatigue and dehydration, he was given more strychnine, two egg whites, and a swallow of brandy. His body was sponged with water warmed on the boiler of a steam automobile; more brandy was given. Led to the viewing boxes to receive the victory cup from David Francis, he was too weak to accept it. He had lost eight pounds during the race and never again competed. (Missouri Historical Society.)

A sober group escorts an exhausted, dehydrated, and slightly poisoned Thomas Hicks to the Physical Culture Building for his medical examination. The medical team announced that "... Hicks' vitality was very low." (Missouri Historical Society.)

Thomas Hicks, winner of the marathon, rests outside of the Physical Culture Building after recovering from his ordeal. (Missouri Historical Society.)

David Francis, president of the Louisiana Purchase Exposition and of the Olympic Games, commissioned this trophy for the winner of the marathon. (Bennitt.)

Thomas Hicks, fully recovered, poses with the gold medal pinned to his jersey, next to the marathon trophy, donated by David Francis, and the victory cup. (Lucas.)

Five

Aquatic Events

Newspapers provided images of the local teams competing in the Olympic rowing events. Western Rowing Club members, above, and the Mound City Four, beside their craft, competed in the coxless four event. The men in the single sculls, wearing variations in team jerseys, represent the Century Boat Club. Rowing and sculling took place on Creve Coeur (French for heartbreak) Lake northwest of the Fair grounds. (*St. Louis Post Dispatch.*)

Spectators line the shore, watching the finish of the second heat of the 100-yard freestyle. The pole with the barrel float in the middle, tied to the flagged uprights, marks the finish line. Judges in the small boat record the times and order of finish. The trolley that carried fairgoers to and from the grounds waits behind the crowd. (Missouri Historical Society.)

Finalists in the 100-yard free style swimming race prepare to dive into the U.S. Life Saving Exhibit Lake. Zoltan von Halmay of Hungary beat his five American competitors with a time of 1 minute, 2.8 seconds, swum in a straight course, point to point. An amateur photographer, in a bathing suit, snaps a picture from the bow of the life saving boat. (Missouri Historical Society.)

Hungarian swimmer Zoltan von Halmay, a double gold medalist, won the 50- and 100-yard freestyle events. The gentleman next to him is an unidentified Hungarian official. (St. Louis Public Library, Special Collections.)

The Hungarian representatives are photographed on the life saving exhibit dock. Franz Kemeny (3), a member of the International Olympic Committee, leads the delegation. Swimmer Zoltan von Halmay (6) was a double gold medalist in the 50- and 100-yard freestyle, and Geza Kiss (7) won a bronze medal for the 880-yard freestyle and a silver for the one-mile freestyle. (Missouri Historical Society.)

Four wet swimmers and an official of the New York Athletic Club stand on the dock in front of one of the life saving exhibit boats. Charles M. Daniels, second from left, was the most successful, winning gold medals in the 220 and 440-yard freestyle events, capturing a silver in the 100-yard freestyle, and taking home a bronze in the 50-yard freestyle. (Missouri Historical Society.)

As the starter fires his pistol, swimmers in the 440-yard race dive into the Life Saving Exhibit Lake. The portable dock is buoyed on barrels, making for a less than stable push off. Charles Daniels of the New York Athletic Club, second from left, won the gold medal. (Missouri Historical Society.)

Charles Daniels poses for the photographer after winning the 440-yard freestyle race. Daniels won four medals for swimming: gold for this event and for the 220-yard freestyle, silver for the 100-yard freestyle, and bronze for the 50-yard freestyle. (Missouri Historical Society.)

German Georg Zacharis leads in the 440-yard breaststroke; no other swimmers are in view. Zacharis won the gold in this event and bronze in the 100-yard backstroke. (St. Louis Public Library, Special Collections.)

Emil A. Rausche of Germany poses for the camera after winning the one-mile freestyle championship. Rausche won the gold medal for this event, as well as the 880-yard freestyle, and won a bronze for the 220-yard freestyle. (Missouri Historical Society.)

These spectators paid 10¢ each to watch members of the U.S. Coast Guard demonstrate "life saving techniques at sea." The man-made U.S. Life Saving Exhibit Lake was on the west side of the fairgrounds, between the Ferris Wheel and the Great Floral Clock. In addition to the daily life saving demonstrations, the Olympic swimming and diving events were held here. (St. Louis Public Library, Special Collections.)

Edgar H. Adams of the New York Athletic Club leaves the diving block in the plunge-for-distance event. Adams came in second to teammate Bill Dickey, with a distance of 57 feet, 6 inches. Adams also competed in the 220-yard freestyle, the 880-yard freestyle, and the one-mile freestyle, but only medaled in the plunge. (Missouri Historical Society.)

William P. Dickey of the New York Athletic Club won his only event in the plunge for distance. Swimmers dove and without propelling themselves with arms, legs, or upper body, glided as far as possible under water. Distance was measured where a swimmers face emerged or to his position at the end of 60 seconds. Each competitor had three attempts. Dickey glided 62 feet, 6 inches, 5 feet beyond second place. (Missouri Historical Society.)

Dr. George H. Sheldon of St. Louis demonstrates his flair at fancy diving in this photograph by Jessie Tarbox Beals. Sheldon was in a class of his own in the fancy diving competition, and all agreed he was by far the best performer. (Missouri Historical Society.)

Frank Kehoe of the Chicago Athletic Club tied with Alfred Braunschweiger of Germany for third in the fancy diving. Kehoe received the bronze medal when Braunschweiger refused to compete in a tie-breaking match. (Missouri Historical Society.)

Kehoe displays his third-place form in the fancy dive competition. The fancy dive was the only event in the diving competition. (Missouri Historical Society.)

The Chicago Athletic Club swimming team poses on the lifesaving boathouse. Their jerseys vary slightly; some have adjustable straps. Captain David T. Hammond repaired his with a pin, pulling his suit askew and exposing a nipple. Frank Kehoe, #9, won the bronze in the 50-yard freestyle. The man in the striped trousers is E.C. Brown, chairman of the Athletic Commission of the Chicago Athletic Association. (Missouri Historical Society.)

Alfred Braunschweiger of Germany tied for third place in the fancy diving with American Frank Kehoe. A "dive-off" was scheduled by officials, but the Germans, convinced that their man had out-performed his competitor, lodged a protest and Braunschweiger refused to compete. (Missouri Historical Society.)

Six

Weightlifting, Gymnastics, and Wrestling

Two-handed weight lifting was one of only two weight lifting events. Only the United States and Greece participated. Perikles Kakousis easily bested the three Americans, lifting 246.25 pounds. Second place finisher Oscar Osthoff lifted only 186 pounds. Weight lifting, considered part of track and field, took place outside in the stadium infield. The suited gentleman to the left is the announcer C.J. Harvey. (Missouri Historical Society.)

Perikles Kakousis in action on his way to winning the gold in the two-handed weightlifting event. Evaluating him is event judge and noted Canadian artist, doctor, and physical educator, R. Tait McKenzie. Kakousis was the only Greek to compete in weightlifting. (Missouri Historical Society.)

Perikles Kakousis lifts 246.25 pounds to win the gold medal in the two-handed weightlifting competition. He and the judges are on the sandy surface of the stadium infield; the Physical Culture Building is in the background. (Bennitt.)

Perikles Kakousis of the Athens Pan-Hellenic Athletic Club beat three Americans to win the two-handed weightlifting competition. Kakousis, 24, was also a member of the Greek tug-of-war team. (Missouri Historical Society.)

Oscar Paul Osthoff of the Milwaukee Athletic Club stands on the stadium infield, suited up for the weightlifting competition. Osthoff, in some sources misidentified as Otto C., won a silver medal in the two-handed lift. He won the gold for the All-Around Weightlifting championship with a come-from-behind victory in the tenth and final event by wowing the judges with handstand pushups. (Missouri Historical Society.)

Oscar Paul Osthoff, Olympic weightlifting champion, stands in the infield looking awkward and uncomfortable in a suit, tie, and cap. (Missouri Historical Society.)

Frederick Winters of New York is seen here winning the one-handed dumbbell lift. The weight, 126.5 pounds, is painted on one sphere of the soldered, one-piece dumbbell. This event was one of ten that determined the All-Around Weight Lifting Olympic Champion; Winters was second over all, winning a silver medal. (Missouri Historical Society.)

Frederick Winters poses holding a barbell and, tired of bruises, wears unique baseball catcher-like shin guards. Winters won six All-Around Weightlifting events, leading after nine events by 5 points. The final event was a competitors-choice freestyle, and up to 25 points were awarded. Winters chose one-hand push-ups, but judges were more impressed by Oscar Osthoff's handstand push-ups. Winters earned 7 points, but Osthoff got 15 and the gold. (Missouri Historical Society.)

This model gymnasium exhibit, with equipment provided by the A.G. Spalding Company, is set up in the Physical Culture Building. The photograph is taken from the elevated running track that circles the room. Gymnastic rings and climbing ropes hang from the steel beams. Radiators provide steam heat and light comes in through large skylights. Gymnastic events were the first Olympic competitions, held on July 1 and 2. In 1904, gymnastics included six events: the parallel bars, the high bar, the side and long horse; plus three events now considered part of track and field: the 100-yard run, the shot put, and the long jump. (Missouri Historical Society.)

A state-of-the-art adjustable vaulting horse sits with its mat and springboard inside the Physical Culture Building gymnasium. The thick tufted matts and new equipment on display was kept pristine, while the Olympic competitors used an older model four-legged horse. Horizontal bars, climbing ropes, adjustable sit-up boards, and racks of Indian clubs are in the background. (Missouri Historical Society.)

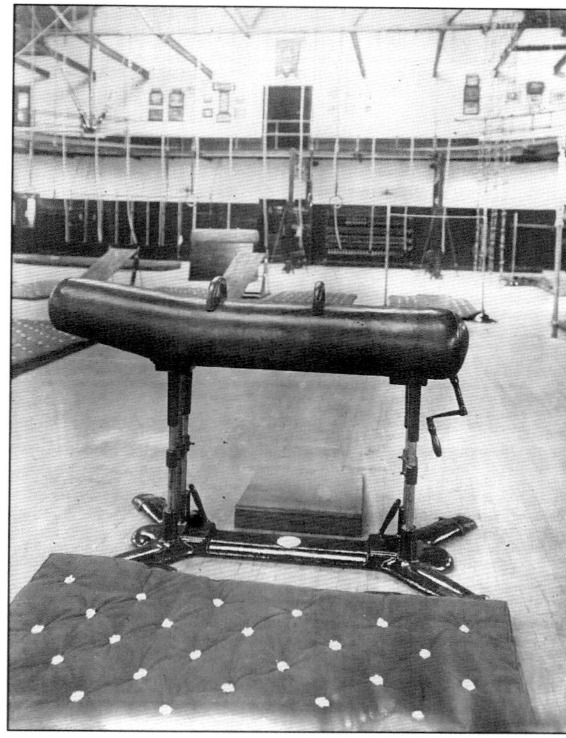

Adjustable parallel bars, pictured here in front of vaulting horses and a badminton net, were part of the A.G. Spalding Company exhibit of athletic equipment. The parallel bars actually used outside in competition were cruder looking than this new example. (Missouri Historical Society.)

An unknown athlete performs on the parallel bars as other gymnasts watch. Their attire resembles contemporary baseball uniforms, with short belted trousers, collared long-sleeve shirts, and high socks. In the 1904 Olympics, gymnastics included three track and field events; athletes competing in all of the events to determine an overall champion. (Missouri Historical Society.)

An unidentified gymnastics team poses in front of the stadium stands. Each wear matching sleeveless shirts and yachting-style caps, but the rest of the uniform apparently came from home. (Missouri Historical Society.)

An unidentified gymnast is set to perform on the high bar. Only a few spectators watch from the stadium seats, and the judge in the Panama hat rocks back in his chair. (Missouri Historical Society.)

Anton Heida of the Philadelphia Turnverein (gymnastics club) performs a handstand on the high bar during the individual combined exercise event. Heida won the gold in this competition, which also included parallel bars, the long horse, and side horse. With his help, the Philadelphia Turnverein won the overall team gymnastic championship. (Bennitt.)

The German gymnastics team is immaculately decked out, from the straw boaters in their hands to the matching belts and socks. Only one maverick has on a short-sleeved jersey. The dapper man on the far left also appears with the German swimming team. (Missouri Historical Society.)

A gymnast performs a dismount. The mat sits directly on the sand in the pit. Vaulting horses and parallel bars wait in the background while athletes watch another competition. At least the judges are watching the gymnast. (Missouri Historical Society.)

Gymnasts race down a track in lanes divided by white cord strung on iron range pins. The Ferris Wheel is just visible in the background. (Missouri Historical Society.)

Five gymnasts take part in a running event while an observation balloon ascends from the aeronautical grounds behind the tall wind screens in the distance to the left. (Missouri Historical Society.)

The official in the dark suit and derby has just fired the starting pistol, and a group of gymnasts from various teams takes off. (Missouri Historical Society.)

Three gymnasts stride toward the finish line. These runners appear, from their uniforms, to be members of the same team. (Missouri Historical Society.)

An unidentified gymnast throws the shot, watched by officials in suits and straw hats and athletes in modified baseball-style uniforms with rolled-up or cut-off trousers. (Missouri Historical Society.)

Otto F. Roehm, temporarily on his head, represents the Buffalo Central YMCA in the 145-pound wrestling match. Roehm, 22, managed to right himself and defeat Rudolph Tesing of the St. George's Athletic Club of New York. (Bennitt.)

Charles F. Erickson, 29, representing the Brooklyn Norwegian Turnverein, defeats William Beckman of the New Westside Athletic Club of New York in the 158-pound match. (Bennitt.)

Boys Club of New York representative Benjamin J. Bradshaw, 25, wins the 135-pound match from Theodore J. McLean of the National Turnverein of Newark, New Jersey. (Bennitt.)

Seven

Archery, Lacrosse, Tennis, and Golf

Mrs. Lida Scott Howell, far left, dominates this team photograph of the Cincinnati Archers, just as she dominated women's archery. Mrs. Howell won the gold in both individual events in St. Louis and was 17-time American ladies' archery champion. This was the only event in which women competed. (Bennitt.)

Four mature gentlemen, with their long bows, pose by a target. The archer on the left wears an arm guard. Celebrating his 64th birthday the day before the competition, Galen Carter Spencer became the oldest American Olympic gold medalist ever when his team, the Potomac Archers of Washington, won the men's team round event. A member of the second place team in the same event, 68-year-old Samuel Duvall of the Cincinnati Archers became the oldest American to win any Olympic medal. These two age records still stand. (Missouri Historical Society.)

George Philip Bryant, with finger tabs on his right hand and a guard on his left arm, concentrates on the target. Bryant dominated the men's archery competition, finishing first in the two individual events and winning the bronze as a member of the Boston Archers in team competition. (Bennitt.)

Beals C. Wright of Boston was the star of Olympic tennis, winning gold medals for both singles and, with Edgar Leonard, doubles. His father, George Wright, was an exceptional professional baseball player while his uncle, Harry Wright, was an innovator in professional baseball organization, achieving national acclaim as "the father of the professional game." (St. Louis Public Library, Special Collections.)

Dwight F. Davis, 25, demonstrates his serving technique. Davis, a wealthy St. Louis resident and champion lawn tennis player, had announced his "retirement" from tennis in 1903. The following year he came out of retirement to compete in the Olympic singles and doubles matches, but lost in the second round of both events. (St. Louis Public Library, Special Collections.)

Edgar W. Leonard of Boston tied for third in the singles competition, and, teamed with Beals Wright, won the gold in the doubles competition. Tennis was played on dirt courts adjacent to the stadium. (Bennitt.)

In 1899, Dwight Davis, a self-confident Harvard senior, had contacted the president of the U.S. Lawn Tennis Association offering to sponsor an international tennis trophy. Winning the Davis Cup is still one of the highest achievements in international competition. Davis later entered politics, then volunteered for service in Word War I, achieving the rank of Lt. Colonel and winning the Distinguished Service Cross for extraordinary heroism. One of the founders of the American Legion, Davis was Secretary of War in the Coolidge administration, Governor General of the Philippines under Hoover, and briefly considered for the Republican presidential nomination in 1928. (Missouri Historical Society.)

Alphonzo E. Bell of Los Angeles teamed with Robert Leroy to capture the silver medal in doubles competition. Bell also competed in singles play, tying for third. (Bennitt.)

Japanese tennis champion Shunzo Tokaki traveled to St. Louis to study American athletic methods and was expected to compete in the Olympic tennis tournament. In early July, he lost to Ralph McKittrick in the Missouri State Championship tournament and did not appear in September to compete in the Olympics. (*St. Louis Post-Dispatch.*)

These images of the Winnipeg, Manitoba Shamrocks, a Canadian lacrosse team, appeared in the *Chicago Tribune*. On their way to St. Louis, the Shamrocks stopped in Chicago to play an exhibition game with that city's best lacrosse team, easily beating them 14–5. Three of the players pictured were on the squad that won the Olympic gold medal: L.H. Pentland, upper left; William Burns, bottom center; and W. Brennach, lower right. Trainer H. Sullivan is in the lower left, wearing the checkered jersey. (*Chicago Tribune*.)

Henry Chandler Egan, here dressed in knickers, billed cap, and tucked-in tie, was a month past his 20th birthday when he won the U.S. Amateur Championship just a week before the Olympic golf competition. He was favored to win the gold medal. After five days of golf, playing 36 holes each day, the young American was thought to have a physical advantage over his 46-year-old Canadian opponent. But Egan not only lost; after the match he retired to bed, exhausted. (*St. Louis Post-Dispatch.*)

SUNDAY WANT DIRECTORY

ST. LOUIS POST-DISPATCH

SUNDAY WANT DIRECTORY

Lyon of Canada Wins the Olympic Golf Championship

EAGAN LOST THREE UP AND TWO TO PLAY ON RAIN-SOAKED GREENS

CARD OF THE FINAL MATCH

EGAN SAYS HE WAS "OVERGOLFED"

LYON ATTRIBUTES VICTORY PRINCIPALLY TO LONG DRIVES

By G. S. LYON

CHOICE OF STUDIES NOT FOR STUDENTS

DREAM BOOK FULL OF FAIRY TALES

RECEPTION GIVEN TRAVELERS

JOHN ALEXANDER'S AIRSHIP

"TOO YOUNG, I'M DIVORCED"

DEVOTION COST A FORTUNE

The front page of the September 25 *St. Louis Post-Dispatch* proclaims Canadian George Lyon Olympic golf champion. The 46-year-old began playing golf at the age of 37. A great all-round athlete, he was one of Canada's best cricket batsmen in the 1890s. After defeating 20-year-old Egan, Lyon demonstrated his vitality at the awards dinner by walking the length of the dining room—on his hands! (*St. Louis Post-Dispatch.*)

The gold medal awarded to George Lyon of Canada for individual Olympic golf competition sports a bag of clubs and a thistle, the national flower of Scotland, the country where golf was invented. The golf competition took place at the Glen Echo Country Club, a short train ride from the fairgrounds. (Greensfelder, et al.)

Eight

Place in History

The featured article of the October 1904 *World's Fair Bulletin*, the official publication of the Exposition, highlights the Olympic games and trumpets the accomplishments of the Department of Physical Culture. The vigorous rhetoric of the day describes "the exhibition of physical manhood" and the "bringing together of unquestionably the most scientific body of physical training experts that has ever been assembled." (St. Louis Public Library, Special Collections.)

Frenchman Pierre de Coubertin, father of the modern Olympic games, founded the International Olympic Committee (IOC) in 1894 and orchestrated the first modern Olympics in Athens in 1896. He requested that the term "Olympic" be applied to all sports at the World's Fair, leading to subsequent confusion about what events were officially part of the competition. Coubertin was displeased with the transfer of the Olympics from Chicago to St. Louis, and was also engaged in a personal feud with James E. Sullivan, chief of the Department of Physical Culture. Miffed, he withdrew his personal involvement in the games, and refused to even attend. In his memoirs, 27 years later, Coubertin spitefully denigrated the 1904 Olympics as a failure. (Sullivan.)

President Theodore Roosevelt was honorary President of the Olympic games, but did not attend the opening ceremonies. He was running for re-election and political protocol of the day deemed it unseemly to appear to be campaigning except at purely political events. Roosevelt did welcome the Olympics to America in remarks made from the White House on April 30, the day the Exposition opened, but did not visit the Fair until November 26, after the election and the Olympic competitions were over. Roosevelt watched a football game in the Olympic Stadium between Carlisle and Haskell, the two Indian schools. Baron de Coubertin, in his memoirs, claimed that Roosevelt insisted that the games be held in St. Louis, not Chicago, and had arbitrated the controversy surrounding the choice of host city. No contemporary evidence supports this assertion. (Sullivan.)

James E. Sullivan, chief of the Physical Culture Department and director of the Olympic Games, received a gold medal from Coubertin and the International Olympic Committee for his leadership of the 1904 Games. (Sullivan.)

News and sports photographer Jessie Tarbox Beals prepares for a balloon flight over the fairgrounds. Beals, 33, had worked for two newspapers in Buffalo, but moved to St. Louis expressly to photograph the Fair. Upon her departure from New York, one newspaper reported that "Buffalo lost one of its best professional women today when Mrs. Jessie Tarbox Beals, staff camera artist, departed on an early train for St. Louis." Her work, including panorama views of the Fair from 900-feet high in the balloon, won a gold medal. (Missouri Historical Society.)

A Patagonian (Argentine) throws the javelin during Anthropology Days. (Sullivan.)

A member of the Philippine Moro tribe throws the javelin in an Anthropology Days competition. (Sullivan.)

Chief Antonio of the Pygmy tribe throws a spear during athletic contests for aboriginal peoples. (St. Louis Public Library, Special Collections.)

Only a handful of spectators watch as a "Negrito" participates in the Anthropology Days archery contest. (Sullivan.)

In the Anthropology Days archery competition, an elaborately robed Ainu from Japan takes aim. (Sullivan.)

Members of the Pawnee tribe participate in an archery contest during Anthropology Days. Dressed in traditional garb, one competitor takes aim while others, in a mix of traditional and Americanized clothing, look on. (Missouri Historical Society.)

An African, identified only as Shamba, shoots during the Anthropology Days archery contest. He was defeated by a Cocopa Indian from Mexico and an Ainu from Japan. (Bennitt.)

A "Negrito" wins the pole climbing event during Anthropology Days. The competitions, held on August 12–13, were organized by Dr. W.J. McGee, chief of the Anthropology Department, and Dr. Simms of the Chicago Field Museum, and were refereed by Dr. Luther Halsey Gulick of New York. (Sullivan.)

Ten runners line up in the stadium at the start of the Anthropology Days one-mile run. None of the participants have been identified, although the event was won by an American Indian, Black White Bear, in a time of 5 minutes 38 seconds. (Sullivan.)

This photograph is identified as a "race between Igorrotes and Moros," both groups from the Philippines. The event was conducted as part of the Philippine Tribal Contests held on September 16. (Bennitt.)

This photograph, originally captioned "Antonio putting the shot," illustrates the Philippine Tribal Contests, one of three athletic competitions held for "savages" during the World's Fair. The other two were called Barbarian Games and Anthropology Days. None were part of the Olympic Games. (Bennitt.)

A tug-of-war contest is held between Sioux, on the right, and Arapaho, on the left, during Anthropology Days. Each team has four members, none of whom seem eager to compete. The Sioux, particularly, are carefully dressed and probably do not relish the possibility of being dragged in the dirt. (Bennitt.)

An unknown individual waves a small American flag. These flags were presented to winners of events during Anthropology Days, while Olympic champions received gold medals. Barely visible in his left thigh are boar bristles, inserted to assist with running. The photographer was Jessie Tarbox Beals. (St. Louis Public Library, Special Collections.)

This plaque on a column of the Francis Field gate memorializes the 1904 Olympics. Universal Exposition was another name for the World's Fair. (Authors.)

The Physical Culture Building built for the 1904 Olympics is now Washington University's Francis Gymnasium. Physical education classes are still taught inside. Outside, ivy and mature trees grace the façade of the 100-year-old building. A large modern addition, not visible in this photograph, is on the right. (Authors.)

This handsome gate leading into the Olympic stadium, renamed Francis Field, was erected in 1914 to honor David R. Francis, president of the Louisiana Purchase Exposition and of the Olympic Games. Located on the grounds of Washington University, the stadium is still used for athletic events. (Authors.)